MW00893648

GENGHIS KHAN

A Life from Beginning to End

Copyright © 2017 by Hourly History.

All rights reserved.

Table of Contents

Introduction

Genghis Khan was a conqueror, leader of armies, and founder of an empire. He waged a long war with the kingdoms of China that the Chinese credit with eventually laying the foundations for unity of their country. He destroyed two entire empires, leaving so little of one nation in western China behind that only traces can be found today. Under Genghis, Mongols reached toward the West, carrying exploratory raids as far east as Russia and Georgia. He re-arranged Mongol society and commanded absolute loyalty from his followers.

Yet this formidable figure—the Khan who rode boldly at the front of his troops on their fast and sturdy Mongolian horses, used the element of surprise to strike his enemies fiercely, and killed all who resisted without mercy—is not a complete one. Genghis' story is that of a boy born under a different name ("Genghis Khan" is only a title), a boy who encountered difficulty, struggled through poverty, and had to escape from enemies even at a young age. Later, it is the story of a leader who learned from his enemies and successfully adapted his methods of warfare to meet new challenges, as well as who had to set up unprecedented Mongol systems of administration and bureaucracy. Once, legend has it, Genghis even met a unicorn.

Genghis Khan's influence was even wider than the empire he built, and his history survives in an abundance of primary sources. Many of these come from China, while others come from Arabic, European, or Persian historians. But among these sources, one stands out. *The Secret History of the Mongols*, written in the thirteenth century, is a classic, the Mongolian language's oldest literary work. Many of the stories about Genghis come from *The Secret*

History, which strives more to show the Khan as a ruler and a leader than to give the details of his military strategies. And while the exact truth about parts of Genghis' life, as with many ancient historical figures, is sometimes in question, here you will discover the details that add up to a big picture—an image of the rise and rule of a leader who changed his world and ours.

Chapter One

Poverty and Captivity

"Apart from our shadows we have no friends."

—Hoelun in The Secret History of the Mongols

By the end of the first century CE, the Mongols roamed and thrived on the wide, grassy steppes of central Eurasia. These nomads relied heavily on their sturdy horses as they hunted, fought, and herded other animals—sheep, goats, and cattle. They had developed a unique way of life, dwelling in domed tents called *gers* and carrying composite bows made of wood, horn, and sinew. These bows were much more powerful even than the famed English longbows. Around 800 CE, Mongols began to move into the valley of the Onon River, in the eastern part of modern Mongolia. Though it would take 400 years more to come about, the valley these nomads pioneered would become the birthplace of the man who would raise the Mongols up from obscurity to immense power.

Genghis Khan, whose title was probably pronounced closer to the transliteration from old Mongolian, "Chinggis," was the descendant of several great Mongol chiefs. Genghis' grandfather, in fact, was the first to call himself by the title "Khan." But around the time of Genghis' birth, which scholars uncertainly place near 1162 CE, the Jin dynasty of China scored a major victory over their nomadic Mongol neighbors. The Mongols, who had been temporarily unified under Genghis' great-grandfather

Kabul, were left without a leader and quickly sunk into the poverty and chaos of warring clans.

Genghis' father, Yesugei, was one of the leaders of a clan known as the Borjigins. He worked to create alliances with several of his neighbors, including a Turkic tribe called the Keraits. According to *The Secret History of the Mongols*, Yesugei caught sight of a beautiful woman being driven in an enclosed cart by her husband, Chiledu. With the help of his brothers, Yesugei attacked, drove Chiledu away, and stole the young bride named Hoelun for himself. The practice of bride-stealing was not uncommon in the culture of the steppes at the time, and Hoelun had no choice but to become Yesugei's wife. But Chiledu's tribe, the Merkits, would long remember the offense and would later seek revenge.

When Hoelun gave birth to a son, Yesugei named the boy (who would later become Genghis) Temujin. This name is sometimes said to derive from the word for iron, *tömör*. This etymology, however, is likely a myth. Whatever the meaning of the name, its source is clear: Yesugei named his son after a recently captured Tatar enemy, following a cultural tradition. *The Secret History* tells us that Temujin was born clutching a clot of blood in his hand. This was interpreted as a sign of power, though the interpretation may have been made in retrospect. From the time of his birth, Temujin's family claimed he had "fire in his eyes and light on his face"—an idiom meaning that he was destined for fame.

Temujin's beginnings may have appeared propitious, but his life was soon to take a downward turn. When Temujin turned eight, his father arranged for him to be betrothed to a girl a year older than him named Börte. Börte was from Hoelun's original clan, the Ongirads. Yesugei left Temujin with the Ongirads and embarked on the journey home. As he traveled, he stopped to accept the hospitality of a band of Tatars. Just days later, he arrived home terribly ill and soon died, but not before sending for Temujin to return. Many accused the Tatars of poisoning him; they were a group among whom Yesugei had made numerous enemies through raids.

Whether the Tatars were guilty or not, Yesugei was dead. His brothers and relations abandoned Hoelun and her six children (four of whom were her own and two who were Yesugei's children by an unknown second wife). In a culture where a male protector was relied on to provide safety and support for his family, Hoelun and her children's situation was desperate. They were left without the herds that provided essentials such as meat, milk, and felt to the nomads. Temujin, his mother, and his siblings survived by becoming hunter-gatherers. They fished in the Onon River and searched for fruit and edible roots.

These years of poverty and struggle were not wholly uneventful. First, Temujin made friends with a boy named Jamukha. The boys became so close that they made promises binding each other as blood brothers; they had no way of knowing the repercussions this friendship would have on their future lives. Then, when Temujin was 13, another fateful event occurred. After a quarrel with his half-brother, Begter, Temujin was unsatisfied by Hoelun's attempts to make peace between the boys. She pointed out that the family was alone in the world and had no one to rely on except one another, but Temujin did not listen to her words. Instead, bearing a grudge, he coerced his younger brother Kasar into helping him kill Begter. Hoelun was horrified, and her forceful denunciation of Temujin and Kasar caused Temujin to finally see what he had not— the importance of familial allegiance, loyalty, and co-operation in a world where they could depend on no one else.

Before long, Temujin would face a challenge greater than the subsistence living his family had endured for years. Some of Yesugei's relatives, a tribe called the Taychiuts, attacked the camp where Temujin, Hoelun, and the siblings were living. Temujin escaped the camp, hiding in the forest for nine days. But at last, desperate with hunger, he was forced to surrender himself to his enemies. The Taychiuts moved Temujin from place to place, always wearing a wooden device called a *cangue* that fastened to his neck and wrists and had a rope for his captors to lead him. Things did not look good for the young man until one night he found himself in the tent of a man named Sorkan-shira. Sorkan-shira was originally of another clan and not entirely loyal to his Taychiuts. He let Temujin sleep a bit more comfortably by loosening his cangue.

Soon after, on the evening of a festival, Temujin saw his chance to make an escape. Most of the tribe was distracted or drunk, and only one young man guarded Temujin. He yanked the rope out of the youth's hands and took off. Knowing that his captors would be mobilized to give chase before long, Temujin made his way to the nearby Onon River. He found a shallow cove and lay down in the water with only his head, held by the cangue, still above the surface. The hunters streamed by, not looking in the water—except Sorkan-shira. Sorkan-shira, however, was really on his way home, not a serious participant in the search. He saw Temujin, but rather than revealing the escapee, he delayed and distracted the searchers until late in the night. When the searchers at last gave up, Sorkan-shira alerted Temujin that it was safe to leave the water and return to his family.

But Temujin, still bound by the cangue and in desperate condition after having spent hours lying in freezing water, knew that he would be unable to travel all the way back to his family's camp. So instead, he followed the direction

Sorkan-shira had taken until he found the man's ger. Sorkan-shira was far from happy to see the fugitive enter his tent and tried dispel the dangerous situation by sending him off immediately into the frigid night. But Sorkan-shira's wife and sons intervened to help Temujin, removing the cangue, helping him get dry, and finally, hiding him in a cart full of wool where he could sleep. The hunt for the escapee resumed the next day, and the searchers even began to look in tents.

When they came to Sorkan-shira's ger, the *Secret History* tells, they searched the tent thoroughly and then began to look in the cart. But just before they uncovered Temujin's foot, Sorkan-shira interrupted. He pointed out that no one could lie under a heap of wool in the heat of the day. The searchers, believing this argument, left the tent. After this close call, Sorkan-shira provided Temujin with food and a horse and hurried him away. Temujin managed to return to his family, but he did not forget that Sorkan-shira and his sons had helped him at a point of great need; later, when Genghis began to rise from obscurity to power, he would reward these men who had aided him in escaping captivity.

Chapter Two

Becoming a Leader

"On Sacred Khaldun

I was a louse

But I escaped

And my life was spared."

—*Temujin in The Secret History of the Mongols*

By the time Temujin was 15, his family had begun to regain their footing in the world, though they remained far from wealthy. They had some herds again, and they had nine horses as well. As a young man, Temujin took up the role of the protector of his family and the animals that provided his family's livelihood. When thieves stole eight of their horses, Temujin was resolute that he must go after the thieves on the remaining horse. After two days of tracking, following the thieves, he came to a camp and a herd of horses. There he met a young man close in age to himself, Boorchu. Boorchu had seen the thieves drive Temujin's horses by the camp, and he immediately decided to join Temujin. He even replaced Temujin's tired horse with a new one.

After three days of riding companionably together, the two teenagers discovered the thieves' camp and herds. Temujin's horses were there among the thieves' animals, so the boys quickly rode in, separated them from the herd, and headed out again with the reclaimed horses. Only one man gave chase, but Temujin pulled out his bow and fired an arrow back at the man, who disappeared. The two boys successfully recovered the animals and took them back to Boorchu's camp. There, they were met by Boorchu's father, who had not known where his son had gone and had assumed the worst—that Boorchu had died out on the steppes. Finding his son alive and well, Boorchu's father affirmed the new friendship of the two young men.

Temujin offered Boorchu some of the recovered animals, but his friend refused, saying that he already had enough and could not accept a reward for a deed done for the sake of friendship. Boorchu and Temujin's friendship would stand the test of time, and Boorchu would eventually become one of the most important generals of the future Genghis Khan's great armies.

As he took up his role as an adult, Temujin decided it was time to act on the betrothal that had been made when he was only a child. At 16, he traveled to meet the Ongirads again and married Börte amid great celebration. She brought to the marriage an impressive dowry of a magnificent black sable gown. Now married, Temujin's status increased as he became the official head of the family. He had strong allies in his brothers, his friend Boorchu, and Börte's clan.

But Temujin knew that to increase his power and status, he would need more allies than this. Therefore, he looked to a natural place—Toghrul, the leader of a powerful people known as the Keraits, whose influence stretched from Mongolia and into the Gobi Desert. Toghrul had been not only a friend of Temujin's father, Yesugei, but the two had even taken oaths of brotherhood. With his brother Kasar and one of his half-brothers, Temujin journeyed to meet Toghrul. He hoped that the ruler would look kindly on the son of his friend. When this was not enough to win him Toghrul's assistance, Temujin brought out an item of great value: the sable gown that had been Börte's dowry. With this expensive gift, he secured the help of the Keraits in reuniting the Mongols.

As Temujin's reputation began to grow, news about the ambitious young man began to spread. Some of this news made its way to unfriendly ears. The Merkits, the people from whom Yesugei had stolen his bride so many years before, heard of the growing strength of young Temujin. Though Chiledu, Hoelun's original husband, had died, his brother Chilger still lived and wanted revenge. The Merkits gathered a large raiding party to attack the camp where Temujin's family was living. Most of the family escaped, but somehow Börte and an old servant named Koagchin were left behind. Koagchin hid Börte in a covered cart and tried to drive away. But when the cart broke down, it drew the Merkits attention. Looking in the back, Temujin's enemies discovered Börte and took her captive, giving her as a wife to Chilger.

Temujin himself had fled into the hills to escape capture. *The Secret History* tells how, after days of hiding and wandering, he found himself safe and on the most sacred mountain of his people, Burkhan Khaldun. He later used this deliverance to claim for himself a place as a ruler ordained by heaven, helped by the power of the divine even before his rise to success.

Now, having escaped from his would-be captors, Temujin faced the task of rescuing his wife. He would need the help of his allies, most especially Toghrul. The leader of the Keraits came through, keeping his promise by sending a significant amount of cavalry to Temujin's aid. Temujin also called upon an old friend, that of his boyhood companion Jamukha. Jamukha had been held captive by the Merkits but had escaped, rising to become a leader in his clan. Now he, too, answered Temujin's call for aid, interested in not only helping his friend but also exacting revenge on his former captors.

Between Temujin, Toghrul, and Jamukha, a force of thousands of men and horses was mobilized to march against the Merkits. The Merkits, seeing the armies approaching, dispersed and fled. Temujin, riding through his fleeing enemies, shouted Börte's name. Börte was being carried away in a cart but jumped out of the moving vehicle when she heard Temujin. Upon finding Börte, Temujin ended the raid, having done what he had come for. His reputation as a leader only increased. Unfortunately, when Börte's first child was born, her captivity made the boy's father uncertain. As a consequence, this child, Jochi, could not become Temujin's heir.

After this triumph against the Merkits, Temujin and his people camped together with Jamukha's family for a time. The two men exchanged gifts and appeared to be devoted companions, spending much of their time together. But after about 18 months, something changed. Jamukha suggested that the two should camp separately. Temujin was saddened by this suggestion, realizing that separation meant not only a breach in their friendship—if the two were divided, in the competitive world of the steppe, it meant they were rivals for leadership among the Mongols. Temujin acted decisively despite his feelings, removing his family and people and marching through the night to find a new location to make their camp.

The Secret History describes how, after Temujin left Jamukha, some of the lesser families of Jamukha's people followed Temujin and joined him. Over the next ten years, more and more families and clans began to align themselves with the rising leader. Temujin undoubtedly increased the scope of his influence through battle and conquest as well as through voluntary submission. The young leader offered possibility and hope, especially to those who had little other hope of advancement in the world. But it was not only less important families who chose to back Temujin. Even the senior relatives from his clan chose to make him their leader, performing the humbling task of swearing oaths of loyalty to the younger Temujin. They believed that in Temujin, at last, there appeared to be hope for the unification of the Mongol people.

Chapter Three

A Unified People

"If I finish the great work, then I shall share with you men the sweet and bitter; if I break my word, then let me be as the water of the river."

—Genghis Khan in a medieval Chinese biography

Temujin's power was growing, but his challenges among the Mongols were still far from over. Jamukha was a powerful rival with a great following, and he would not just sit by as Temujin became stronger and stronger. Sometime in the 1190s, he marched against Temujin with an army of perhaps more than 20,000. Temujin received a warning in time to escape. Once again, he found himself retreating to hide in the hills near the sacred mountain of Burkhan Khaldun. Surviving this attack, Temujin returned to his people and continued his rise toward greatness.

Around 1200, another battle with Jamukha gave Temujin a chance for victory. Though he had two close calls—once when an arrow killed his horse and a second when a poisoned arrow struck Temujin himself—he not only won the fight but also gained valuable allies and loyal friends. One of his men, Jelme, had cleaned Temujin's wound from the poisoned arrow and risked his life to steal from Jamukha's camp. Another man, Jirko, appeared in Temujin's camp along with the leader's former acquaintance, Sorkan-shira. The two men had been captives of the tribes of Jamukha's confederation, but now had freedom and could unite with Temujin.

Temujin first had a question for the two men: did they happen to know who shot his horse? Jirko, believing in Temujin's value for loyalty and honesty, admitted that he had shot the arrow. He promised to serve Temujin well now that he was free of his captors. Perhaps because of Jirko's honest admission or his companionship with Sorkan-shira, Temujin accepted his offer. He renamed Jirko "Jebe," a name meaning "arrow-point," and declared that he would use Jebe as his arrow. Both Jelme and Jebe would become some of Temujin's most relied-upon generals, two of the four commanders that Temujin called his "hounds."

Despite this one victory for Temujin, Jamukha still ruled many tribes. In addition, a new problem arose. Temujin's previous valuable alliance with Toghrul presented difficulties as the old man began to lose his grip on those he ruled. Temujin assisted Toghrul by sending four powerful warriors to rescue the man's family when they were captured in a battle, and as a response of gratitude, Toghrul proposed marriage between their children. But Toghrul's son, Senggum, not wanting Temujin to gain greater control over the clan, resisted this idea. Senggum encouraged his father to turn against Temujin. Jamukha, too, sent messages to Toghrul, urging him to act to stop Temujin's growing power. Toghrul found himself torn between loyalty to Temujin, his ally and the son of his sworn blood-brother, and loyalty to his son Senggum. As a result, Toghrul at first did nothing.

Senggum could not stand to watch Temujin take power, so he turned to other strategies. He invited Temujin to marry his sister after all, but the invitation was a trap. Senggum intended to take the opportunity to kill Temujin. Luckily Temujin was warned in time and turned around. Seeing his plan failing, Senggum pursued Temujin and forced a battle. Temujin, unprepared for this, only just managed to escape with a small group of men and retreated into hiding along a lake or a river. This was a low point for Temujin, as he knew his enemies banded together against him. His own forces were much more scattered.

But despite the unpropitious outlook, this moment became one of famed legend. Though *The Secret History* does not record it, many other documents, even from less than a hundred years after Genghis Khan's life, describe the scene. As Temujin hid with his men, the small group endured great hardship together. They had no food, and the only water available was the muddy river or lake by which they camped. In the midst of this hardship, Temujin made a promise of loyalty to his men, that they would share together both the suffering and the glory and rewards of his campaign.

The men survived their wilderness ordeal, and Temujin decided to wait and gain strength before acting. As he waited, the coalition against him began to fall apart. Jamukha had never been a man of great patience, and not seeing his ends gained, he decided to assassinate Toghrul. Toghrul learned of the plot and evaded it. At this moment of division and weakness, Temujin struck. His battle with Toghrul's forces lasted three days. At last, Toghrul, Senggum, and Jamukha all fled. Toghrul and Senggum met their deaths in their attempts to escape, but Jamukha found asylum with a people group to the west, the Naimans.

Because Jamukha lived, another battle was inevitable. Jamukha, with his Naiman allies, was well prepared for battle. Temujin marched across the plains to meet him in 1204. But the long journey left both Temujin's men and horses exhausted, in no state to immediately launch into a battle. One of Temujin's generals came up with a clever idea to buy them more time. When night fell, each man lit not just one, but five fires. Jamukha's scouts went back to report that Temujin's army was massive. Though the opposing forces were stopped from attacking that night, the delay did not last as long as Temujin and his men might have hoped.

Tayang, the leader of the Naimans, heard the report from the scouts and wanted to retreat. But his son Kuchlug taunted his father and convinced him to go through with the attack. The battle took place about 200 kilometers away from where Ulaanbaatar, the capital of modern Mongolia, now stands. Despite their lack of rest, somehow Temujin's armies managed to pull off a great victory. Tayang was killed, but his son Kuchlug escaped. Jamukha, too, escaped and tried to find sanctuary with the Merkits, Temujin's old enemies. Temujin pursued him there and defeated the Merkits. At last, Jamukha was captured through the treachery of his few surviving men. Temujin punished these men for their lack of loyalty to their sworn leader. Then, according to *The Secret History*, he offered a chance for Jamukha, his blood brother, to ask for mercy. But Jamukha refused and was strangled—a noble death since no blood was spilled—and buried honorably.

At long last, Temujin's greatest rival was defeated, and he stood out as the clear leader of all the Mongols. This became official at a national ceremony in 1206, where Temujin received his new title—Genghis Khan. The etymology of this title is unclear to modern scholars. There were other traditional labels for great leaders, such as "Gur Khan," meaning "Universal Khan," which Jamukha had claimed earlier. Some believe that "Genghis" might be related to old Mongolian word for "ocean," *tengis*. The ocean, as well as large lakes, was revered, so this might make sense. In any case, "Genghis Khan" was a new title, one for a man who had consolidated more power among the nomadic peoples of Central Asia than any khan before him.

Chapter Four

The First Campaigns

"I stand here under the protection of Eternal Blue Heaven,
setting all of the people in order."

—*Genghis Khan in The Secret History of the Mongols*

Now that Genghis Khan had brought together not just many of the Mongol clans, but also other nomadic tribes like the Merkits, Keraits, and Naimans, the time had come to look outwards. As the leader of a non-monetized society, Genghis Khan could not pay his armies. Their rewards were the spoils of battle, and he would need to continue his program of conquest to keep the power he had fought so hard for. But even before he could turn his attention to new campaigns, he needed to create a structure for the new society he was establishing.

Traditionally, order among the nomadic peoples came in the form of clans and tribes, but Genghis had started to change that. He gave positions of leadership and power to those who served him well and proved themselves capable and loyal. Sorkan-shira and his sons, who would otherwise never have had hope for a life beyond obscurity, now became Genghis' aides. Jelme, the man who saved Genghis' life and was to become one of his greatest generals, was originally just a blacksmith's son. This new way of appointing leaders helped to undermine the problems of rivalries and divisions that had often caused disunity in the Mongols' tribally ordered society. But it also called for new rules and methods of organization.

For the task, Genghis saw that the keeping of written records would be necessary. He had a captured Naiman administrator, Tatatunga, teach the Uighur script to several men of high status among the Mongols. Then Genghis' adopted brother, Shigi, became the keeper of records, working to develop an official legal code (that is now lost). Genghis also reordered the military, structuring regiments around loyalty to generals rather than to tribes.

As Genghis' administrative work progressed, he was determining the direction of his next conquest. The area of China, in the thirteenth century, was a mixture of nations, languages, religions, and cultures, but three major nations ruled the area. In the northeast, the Jin dynasty controlled the land of Jin. In the southeast stood Song. In the west was Western Xia, home of the Tanguts. This last nation had a remarkable urban culture, with skilled craftsmen, a reliable agricultural base, and a highly developed education system. All of this made Western Xia a rich country—and an ideal target for Genghis Khan since the country was separated from the Mongols by only the empty stretches of the Gobi Desert.

Genghis began his attack on Western Xia in 1209. After marching his troops across the Gobi, his first move was to capture a small town on the outskirts of the country. This prompted the Tanguts to appeal to Jin for help, but the new Jin ruler, Prince Wei, saw no reason to stop a fight between two of his enemies. Genghis and his men continued to push on into Western Xia, following the path of a dry riverbed through the mountains as they marched toward the capital, Yinchuan.

This pass was guarded by a fortress, which held perhaps upwards of 100,000 soldiers. For two months, Genghis' army was stopped. Then they fell back on a tried and true Mongol strategy. Genghis' forces appeared to retreat, leaving just a handful of men on the fields in front of the fortress. When the Tanguts rode out to finish off these men, the rest of Genghis' army, not gone but instead hidden in the nearby foothills, charged out and met them in battle. The Tanguts, no longer having the advantage of their fortress walls, were quickly defeated on the open field. The Mongols marched on towards Western Xia's capital.

Taking the capital proved to be a challenge. The Mongols, with their powerful composite bows and fast horses, were an intimidating force on an open battlefield. But they lacked the heavy and technical equipment usually used for the siege of a city. With their many horses, they would quickly strip the land if they remained in one place too long, and besides this, Western Xia reinforcements were surely on the way. It was essential that Genghis find a way to conquer the city quickly and decisively if he was going to do it at all.

The Mongols looked to the vast system of canals that irrigated the plains where the capital sat. They demolished dams and canal walls, hoping the ensuing flood would drive the city to a desperate surrender. But this idea did not work the way Genghis hoped. The flooding was shallow, stretching across the flat farmland and countryside. The floods succeeded in destroying the Tanguts' crops, but buildings were relatively safe in the shallow waters. On the other hand, the Mongols carts and horses became much less effective, and they had to retreat to a higher elevation. Both the invaders and the Tanguts were left in a bad situation, and so finally the two sides developed a compromise. The Tangut ruler agreed to give extensive tribute, as well as his daughter, to Genghis. In return, the Mongols left, believing that they had turned Western Xia into a submissive vassal. The future would show, however, that this was not quite true.

Though Genghis may have been satisfied with the way his conquest of Western Xia turned out, he was not done with China. The powerful Jin dynasty felt secure in their country of Jin, and they sent messengers commanding Genghis to make ritual obeisance to Prince Wei. The Jin had traditionally collected tribute from many of the nomadic tribes of the steppe. Unsurprisingly, Genghis was having none of this. Genghis had extensive information about the state of Jin, coming from a nomadic tribe on Jin's border, merchants who traveled through Genghis' territory, and Jin officials who deserted their country to join the Mongols. He saw Jin as a weakened state, suffering from recent economic troubles and famine. Still, the Jin did have a significant advantage in sheer numbers.

In 1211 Genghis took his armies across the Gobi once again, this time towards Jin. There, they encountered an important pass, known as the Badger's Mouth, guarded by two huge fortresses. This might have stopped the Mongols, but the general of the Jin forces decided to send a representative out to meet Genghis to negotiate for peace. Unfortunately for the Jin state, this messenger immediately turned traitor and threw in his lot with the formidable Mongol army. He told Genghis where the Jin forces were waiting at the end of the pass. As a result, the Mongols descended on the Jin and devastated their defenses. Bodies lay in piles for 50 kilometers, and the stacks of bones from the battle would still be visible a dozen years later.

Following the great victory at Badger's Mouth, the Mongols fought their way further into Jin. Beijing, the capital, was a well-defended city, so the Mongols turned their attention elsewhere. They sacked and looted across the country. Genghis then sent his general Jebe, his "arrow," against the second most important city in Jin, Mukden (modern Shenyang). As before, the Mongols were unprepared to lay siege to the city. But once again, Jebe made good use of the dependable Mongol strategy of appearing to retreat. He took his men over 150 kilometers away from the city. Mukden's residents, seeing this, were elated. Jebe had even left supplies and baggage behind him, adding to the illusion of a hurried departure. The citizens of Mukden could not believe their good fortune and straggled out of the city, collecting the abandoned supplies and throwing a huge celebration. As they celebrated, they had no idea that Jebe had turned his forces back around. The Mongol troops rode for 24 hours straight and fell upon the now vulnerable, completely open city. It was a smashing victory for Jebe, and by extension, for Genghis.

As the year drew toward a close, Genghis suffered another arrow wound. This was as good a reason as any for the Mongols to withdraw from Jin for a time, enjoying the spoils and plunder of war. They retreated to the grasslands on Jin's border. But this respite for the country of Jin was not destined to last long. By the summer of the next year, the Mongols were ready to invade again. They fought their way through the Badger's Mouth once more, and this time headed toward Beijing. The country was devastated as the Mongols rode through, consuming everything in their path and leaving Jin's citizens without food.

Inside Beijing, chaos reigned. The general who had dramatically lost the battle at the Badger's Mouth the year before, Zhi-zhong, had returned to Beijing and been pardoned by the emperor. Now, as the Mongols neared the city, this general took matters into his own hands. He assassinated the emperor alongside the 500 imperial guards and made himself the regent of the new emperor. Then he sent 6,000 soldiers against the Mongols, warning their commander, Kao-ch'i, that death awaited him should he fail. Not surprisingly, this small force did indeed fail to stop the Mongols, and Kao-ch'i acted to preserve his own life. He fled back to Beijing with a few men, arrived unexpectedly, and assassinated Zhi-zhong. Then he immediately admitted his deed to the emperor. Not unhappy to be out from under the thumb of his controlling regent, the emperor made Kao-ch'i his vice-commander.

In the midst of this political turmoil, Genghis' conquest of the empire had not ceased. He developed alternative methods of taking cities, such as using captured prisoners in the front lines of an assault. The cities' inhabitants, recognizing the prisoners, often surrendered rather than attack their relatives and friends. In this way, the Mongols captured town after town. But Beijing itself was not so easily conquered. It was both well supplied and well defended. The city possessed both powerful crossbows and formidable artillery that was beyond anything the Mongols had. The defenders also had technology on their side—they knew how to use fire and oil to build what was essentially a flame-thrower.

From 1213 to 1214 Genghis pressed the siege of Beijing, even in the face of the Jin advantages and a terrible winter for the Mongols outside the city walls. An entire year of siege did not bode well for those inside Beijing either, so Genghis offered to leave if the emperor would give him tribute. The emperor, desperate to be rid of the Mongol invaders, offered vast amounts of captives, horses, and silk, which Genghis accepted. As the Mongols retreated, the emperor of Jin prepared to move his capital south to a city called Kaifeng, as far away from the plains of the Mongols as he could get.

When Genghis heard of the emperor's undertaking, he was already 400 kilometers north of Beijing, on his way back to the steppes that were home to his people. But the opportunity was too good to pass up. Genghis accused the Jin emperor of not trusting his word and deceiving him. Then he marched his troops right back to Beijing and waited through the fall, winter, and into the spring. In the spring, the Mongols seized the relief supplies that the emperor sent to Beijing. Those in the city began to starve, reportedly resorting to cannibalism. At last, in June, the city surrendered. Genghis himself was not present, having already departed for eastern Mongolia. His men sacked and burned the city. In the wake of Beijing's fall, more towns surrendered to the Mongol force, and millions of refugees escaped towards the south.

Genghis' campaign against Jin was nearly over, but he did not consider it complete as long as the emperor still held out in Kaifeng. Part of Genghis' forces overran Manchuria, invading as far as Korea, where the Korean king offered gifts to placate the Mongols. Then Genghis, with reinforcements from the recently conquered Western Xia, approached Kaifeng. The Mongols and Tanguts fought their way through the heavily fortified area in the midst of winter, pushing forward by around 800 kilometers in only 60 days. Eventually, though, Genghis had to retreat. But this retreat did not mean he was done. The war to subjugate the last of Jin would continue for nearly 20 more years. In the meantime, Genghis would take what he had learned of siege warfare and pursue conquests in another direction— towards the west.

Chapter Five

A Kingdom Once Called Khwarezm

"Let us ride out against the Islamic peoples, to gain vengeance!"

—*Genghis Khan in The Secret History of the Mongols*

To the west of the Mongolian homeland lay the kingdom of Khara Khitai, formed by refugees from eastern China who had subjugated the Muslim inhabitants already living in the area. The kingdom contained what is now Kyrgyzstan as well as pieces of modern Kazakhstan and Tajikistan. It drew Genghis' attention, not because of location or wealth, but because it harbored an old enemy who had begun to grow in strength once again. Kuchlug, the son of the Naiman leader Tayang, had escaped westward after Genghis defeated Tayang years before. Now, in the kingdom of Khara Khitai, Kuchlug was beginning to seize power for himself.

Genghis, seeing Kuchlug as a threat, sent his faithful general Jebe to deal with the situation. Jebe marched thousands of men across the Altai and Tien Shen mountains towards Kuchlug's stronghold of Balasagun. Kuchlug fled before the approaching army, and Jebe pursued him south. At last Jebe and his men caught up to Kuchlug as he headed toward what is now Pakistan. They captured him when Kuchlug made the mistake of turning into a valley that ended in a dead end.

Though Kuchlug was dead and Genghis' long battle with the Naimans was concluded, this hunt brought the Mongols into contact with a kingdom even farther west, the Muslim empire of Khwarezm. Khwarezm was built from the remnants of the earlier great Arabic caliphate and still contained much of the riches of those times. The kingdom's territory covered parts of modern-day Turkmenistan, Uzbekistan, Iran, and Afghanistan. Most important to Genghis, the Silk Road, the famed trading route between east and west, ran through Khwarezm.

According to the records of Muslim historians, Genghis saw Khwarezm as a potentially beneficial trading partner initially. The pattern of invading China had a long precedent among the Mongols, and his conquests to the west in Khara Khitai had been the result of his pursuit of an enemy. Genghis did not have a great motivation to invade beyond the traditional realm of the Mongols, especially when that would mean stretching his borders out in the west while he still conducted a long-term war with the remainder of the Jin in the east.

But unfortunately for the millions who inhabited this western part of Asia, the shah of Khwarezm, named Mohammed, reacted negatively to Genghis' overtures in pursuit of trading relations. Having heard of Genghis' power and his bloody campaigns to the east, Mohammed assumed that Genghis would decide to invade Khwarezm as well. Despite the Mongols' attempts to reassure him, Mohammed took the offensive. He allowed (or perhaps even ordered) a man named Inalchuk, the governor of Otrar, one of Khwarezm's large border cities, to accost the delegation sent by Genghis.

Inalchuk accused the merchants sent by Genghis of being spies and arrested them. Genghis offered Mohammed the chance to recover from this blow to peaceful international relations by giving the ruler the option to deliver Inalchuk for punishment, thereby implying that Inalchuk had acted without Mohammed's knowledge. Instead of taking this last opportunity to secure peace, Mohammed killed at least one of Genghis' ambassadors, and possibly more. He also executed the rest of the trade delegation, between 100 and 450 men. This would prove to be a terrible idea.

Genghis Khan would soon retaliate against Mohammed's insult and challenge. But first, the ruler of the Mongols had an internal issue to deal with: in the event that something happened to him, he needed to settle the question of his heir. Usually, rule passed to the eldest member of a clan, but Genghis, as ruler of much more than a clan, choose to make one of his sons his heir. His first son, Jochi, was of questionable paternity due to his mother's kidnapping by the Merkits. After a fierce argument between Jochi and Genghis' second son, Chagadai, a shaman forcefully reminded the two of the essential importance of family loyalty. They compromised by determining that Genghis' third son, Ogedei, should be his heir.

With this matter decided, the time had come for Genghis to set out westward to avenge the deaths of his trade delegation. In this task, he called for reinforcements from his vassal state, Western Xia. However, the Tanguts thought that Genghis' constant war with the Jin and the development of this new war to the west would keep Genghis from retaliating if they chose to rebel. Instead of sending troops, they sent an insult. They were right about one thing—Genghis was unable to respond to their message with force at that moment. But the Khan swore that Western Xia would one day pay, and he was a man of his word.

In 1219, without the aid of the Tanguts, Genghis marched his army toward the west. Now, the Mongol troops not only relied on the speed of their horses and the strength of their warriors but also transported all the machinery and technology necessary to lay siege to a city. They had learned (and probably captured equipment) from their war with the Jin state. They had also become an army that did not just slaughter their enemy in the usual style of nomadic fighting, but incorporated the captured citizens into their methods of war.

The Mongols first approached the town of Otrar, where Inalchuk had committed his offense. Shah Mohammed, rather than uniting his forces to meet the oncoming threat, kept them separated, scattered among many cities. He was not a popular ruler and uniting his forces would have risked giving enough power to one commander that the Shah himself might be overthrown. The Mongols began a five-month siege of Otrar, which ended when an escaping official accidentally opened a small side gate for the invading army. Genghis' revenge on Otrar was complete as he executed Inalchuk and demolished the city.

Next, Genghis divided his troops, using a pincher movement to squeeze the life out of the kingdom. Jochi led a segment of the army north, while Genghis took his men across the desert toward the major city of Bukhara, in modern Uzbekistan. Small towns in his path, and eventually Bukhara itself, chose to surrender rather than be destroyed by the Mongols. Here at Bukhara, in a sometimes-doubted episode recorded by the Persian historian Juvayni, Genghis may have made a speech in which he declared himself a bringer of punishment ordained by God. Whether this particular story is true or not, Genghis certainly did hold the attitude that his conquests had been divinely decreed by the greatest power the shamanistic Mongols believed in, Eternal Blue Heaven.

Much of Bukhara went up in flames as the Mongols carried away its wealth on their way forward, farther into

Khwarezm. As Genghis propelled his army forward, he sent two generals, Jebe and another man named Subedei, to hunt down Shah Mohammed himself. Mohammed's flight took him all the way to the Caspian Sea, where, on a small island, he died. The two arms of the Mongol army finally met in a city called Urgench (in western Uzbekistan).

The populous city decided to stand up against the Mongols. After five months of fighting, in which the Mongols suffered some serious defeats and then had to fight for the city one small piece at a time, the Mongols came out as the ultimate victors. In retaliation for Urgench's resistance, the Mongol victors killed everyone. According to Juvayni, those who died numbered over a million people. Though this count may be somewhat exaggerated, the massacre at Urgench was not the only one. When combined with the other Mongol mass killings in Khwarezm, such as one that occurred in the city of Merv, the Mongol victory in this Muslim kingdom easily ranks among the world's bloodiest massacres.

Jalal, the son of Shah Mohammed, survived. He continued to spearhead a weak resistance against the Mongols until he eventually was captured. Genghis, according to Juvayni, admired Jalal's bravery and let him go.

Now Genghis was ready to gather his armies and return to his native steppes. He took his men through Afghanistan and into northern India before turning back towards Mongolia. The route was open for Genghis to invade deeper into India, and yet he did not take it. Some sources record that this was because he met a unicorn—perhaps really a rhinoceros. His trusted advisor Chu-tsai—a man who sought religious knowledge by combining the teaching of Confucius, Buddha, and Lao-tzu (founder of Taoism), became the organizer of Genghis' bureaucracy and held great influence over the Khan—interpreted the appearance of this strange animal as a sign to turn back. So the majority of the Mongol army changed direction, turning their attention back towards Mongolia and the never-ending conflict with Jin and Western Xia.

Chapter Six

The Raid Into Europe

"A savage people of Tartars, hellish of aspect, as voracious as wolves in their hunger for spoils, and as brave as lions, have invaded my country."

—Rusudan, sister and heir of King Giorgi of Georgia, in a letter to the Pope

While Genghis led a large portion of his forces back towards their conflicts in the east, some of his generals took a part of the army west. The generals Jebe and Subedei, as well as Genghis' oldest son Jochi, were near the Caspian Sea. They suggested to Genghis that they explore farther into Europe, finding out more particularly about a people called the Bulgars who traded with Khwarezm. These Bulgars were Muslim and separate from the Bulgars who would later lend their name to Bulgaria, though distantly related. So Subedei, Jochi, and Jebe took several thousand troops and began their circling of the Caspian Sea to scout the land for potential further Mongol expansion.

They first appeared in Georgia, conducting a series of raids in which the Mongols quickly proved victorious over the defending Georgians and Armenians. This event had repercussions in Europe, as the Georgians were unable to send aid to the Pope for the attempt to conquer Egypt. Near the Black Sea, the Mongols encountered another enemy, the Cumans. The Cumans were also a nomadic and warlike people, and at first they seemed to be winning against the fewer numbers of the invading Mongols. But the Mongols had many tricks. Jebe and Subedei sent gifts from their Georgian plunder to the Cuman leaders. Satisfied, the Cumans rode away. The Mongols rode after them, capturing small groups left behind and eventually thoroughly defeated the main Cuman army, which was now slowed down with carts, treasures, and siege machines. The Cumans fled toward Russia, while the Mongols took over their territory in the plains north of the Black Sea.

While Jebe stayed behind, protecting a Mongol base for the westward raid, Subedei pushed further into the Crimea. And there, near the Sea of Azov, he met a new people— Europeans. These were Venetians, and they occupied a trading base there. Long interested in westward trade, the Mongols saw an opportunity in the Venetians' access to ships and trade routes. The Venetians, too, saw opportunity in the wealthy and powerful Mongols, with their silk clothes and silver covered saddles. The two parties struck a deal, and the Mongols assisted their new partners by attacking the Black Sea outpost of the Venetians' trading rivals, the Genoese.

As 1222 neared its end, Jebe and Subedei regrouped and continued west. They gathered information as they traveled and hired spies to leave behind for future use. Then they turned northwards in pursuit of the Bulgars. Seeing the Mongols coming their way, the already harried Cumans and some Russian leaders formed a confederation to oppose the invading Mongols. Jebe and Subedei hesitated, hoping that Jochi, still down near the Caspian Sea, would answer their call and join them. He did not. So the Mongols treated with the Russians for peace, claiming they only wanted to fight the Cumans. The alliance of Russian princes responded by killing the Mongol delegation. Now battle between the two forces was inevitable.

The Russian forces and their allies were superior in number, but they lacked the tactical advantage of unity that the Mongols had. The Mongols not only knew how to work together on the field, but were even in touch with Genghis through an express system of riders and horses with frequent exchanges. They may not have looked intimidating to the Russian forces that met them at the Dnieper River, but they were ready for the fight nonetheless. As the Russian cavalry splashed their way across the river, the Mongols met them with only a few arrows before whirling their horses around to run away. The Russians scoffed, feeling confident as they chased the retreating Mongols. As they ran, the Mongols left behind prisoners and livestock, which the Russians collected. The retreat continued for nine days, until May 31. By then, the Russians were beginning to spread out, with the nomadic Cumans in front, and the Russian cavalry, soldiers, and carts and baggage spread out behind. Not surprisingly to anyone familiar with Mongol tactics, this was the moment the Mongols were waiting for. They spun around and made a completely unexpected attack on the dispersed pursuing army.

After this victory over the Russians and their allies, Jebe and Subedei were met by Jochi; the three commanders continued northwards, hunting for the Bulgars. When they encountered the Bulgars, they discovered that these enemies were simply too much. The Mongols, defeated at last in a battle of which little is recorded, turned back toward Mongolia. They would long for revenge in the face of this defeat, but revenge would not happen in Genghis Khan's lifetime. Genghis' hand had reached to its furthest extent, and now his generals rode back to join him in the pressing matter of Western Xia.

Chapter Seven

Keeping Old Promises

"While we eat, let us talk of how we made them die and of how we destroyed them. Let us say: 'That was the end, they are no more.'"

—Genghis Khan in The Secret History of the Mongols

Back in the east, all four major powers—the Mongols, the Tanguts of Western Xia, the Jin, and the Song—were at war. When the young ruler of the Tanguts made a peace agreement with Jin in 1225, Genghis knew he needed to act in order to maintain his supremacy. He crossed the Gobi and the mountains with his men, on his way to deal the long-awaited blow to the Tanguts who had rebelled against him and insulted him years before. However, on the way, Genghis took time to participate in a hunt. He fell from his horse, and an initial injury gave way to illness. Genghis' advisors wanted to stop and wait, but he urged his officials to take another approach. They bought time by sending a message to the Tangut emperor, suggesting that they might be willing to negotiate for peace despite past offenses.

But the emperor's commander-in-chief, Asha, responded with more insults. Now Genghis was furious if he had not been before. He swore that even if he died in the process, he would destroy the Tanguts. He waited until after winter, while his troops hunted and camped in the mountains and some may have even temporarily returned across the desert home.

In the spring of 1227, Genghis was healthy again, and his men were ready for battle. They marched toward the northern city of Khara-Khoto. This fortress was ancient, but against the disciplined and now technologically advanced Mongol troops, it could not stand long. After taking the city, the Mongols used its people and resources to strengthen their armies as they moved forward.

Two more cities surrendered to the advancing Mongols when no reinforcements were forthcoming from the Tangut capital, including one of the Tanguts' most important cities. Then, the Mongols managed a complex crossing of the wide and muddy Yellow River on their way to another key city, Yinchuan. They put Yinchuan under siege, while a part of the Mongol army broke off to capture smaller cities and to stop any possible assistance from Jin. Finally after six months of siege at Yinchuan, Genghis offered to negotiate. The emperor had died and had been replaced by a relative, Xian. Xian asked for time to arrange appropriate gifts for the Khan, and Genghis, not hinting at his true purposes, agreed. In reality, the Tanguts had deceived and insulted the Mongols more than once, and Genghis had no intention of letting them survive. He ordered that the royal line be extinguished.

Seeing the imminent fall of Western Xia, Jin sent ambassadors to the Mongols to work for peace. Genghis, though officially announcing an end to the killing, continued east and marched his army through Jin. Having occupied the western portion of Jin, Genghis obtained a base from which he could finish conquering northern China. But near the southern border of Jin, shared with Song, the Khan became seriously ill. Some scholars speculate that he might have contracted typhus. In any case, his most loyal commanders realized that the disease was serious and took Genghis north again. They hid the severity of his illness from everyone else.

One Chinese source records that even on his deathbed, Genghis still strategized, scheming for the success of his plans for domination. An Arabic scholar later related the Khan's command for his officers to hide his impending death, so that his armies would continue to follow his orders until they were fully carried out and his enemies would not have the chance to take advantage of any Mongol weakness. He left his men with the command to annihilate the Tanguts and perhaps also gave them a plan for continuing the fight against Jin.

When the time came for the Tangut emperor to offer his gifts to Genghis, the emperor was not admitted to Genghis' tent. The official explanation was that Genghis was not well enough to meet with him, but there is also a definite possibility Genghis Khan was already dead. In any case, the Emperor Xian was executed despite his gifts. *The Secret History* records only that Genghis "ascended to heaven"—confirmation of the secrecy with which Genghis' death was guarded. In light of this secrecy, rumors surrounded the story of the Khan's death, claiming he died in different locations or different ways. Some of these stories became more akin to legend and myth than history. But despite (or because of) the uncertainty around the exact time and location of Genghis' death, his commands were carried out. His promise to make Western Xia pay for their treachery was fulfilled—the Mongols destroyed the country, obliterating it so fully that it is generally only familiar to scholars and specialists today.

Conclusion

The location of Genghis' grave, like the details of his death, is uncertain. Two places claim to be the resting place of the famous leader's remains—one in China and one in Mongolia. Myths sprung up surrounding Genghis' burial, as they had his death, with the writings of an Arabic historian and Marco Polo claiming that all who saw the body of Genghis Khan had been immediately killed. While this story seems unlikely, the debate over his final resting place is a small indicator pointing to the continuing legacy of Genghis' life. Genghis laid a foundation for his successors to build upon, and they did. In the next 70 years, under the rule of Genghis' son and his grandson, Kublai Khan, the size of the Mongol Empire doubled. Mongol territory stretched from modern Turkey into Russia and Poland and eastwards to China and Korea. The Mongols were stopped from invading Japan only by terrible storms that crippled their ships.

Though much of the Western world and parts of the Islamic world tend to view Genghis Khan as ruthless and barbaric, nonetheless, books have been written in admiration of his impressive leadership skills. In his homeland, admiration goes further. Mongolia continues to revere Genghis for his ability to bring unity to a dispersed and warring people, a sentiment that especially saw resurgence after the country's departure from communism in the 1990s. Many Mongolians believe that outside writers of history exaggerated the records of Genghis' brutality and downplayed positive attributes of the famed leader.

In China, too, the legacy of Genghis Khan continues. He paved the way for his grandson Kublai to conquer more of China and establish the Yuan dynasty, credited with bringing unity to China. Genghis Khan, the man who rose from poverty to found an empire, lives on in the East as a symbol—in Mongolia, representing independence and a traditional lifestyle; in China, as a representation of ambition and unity.

Made in the USA
San Bernardino, CA
15 August 2020

77062136R00022